But There's So Much DIY in IVF That We Can't Be Sure

Toby Goostree

Fernwood
PRESS

But There's So Much DIY in IVF That We Can't Be Sure

Fernwood Press
Newberg, Oregon
www.fernwoodpress.com

Printed in the United States of America

Page design: Mareesa Fawver Moss
Cover art: Blake Kuhn, Wesley & Roberts.
Author photo: Jolene Mendez

ISBN 978-1-59498-129-6

These intimate poems weave together stories from the book of Genesis, a couple's labyrinthine journey through IVF, and the painful space between wanting and getting what we want. In the "empty circle" ("Anovulation") where conception is a supreme effort, Bible stories of Adam and Eve, Leah and Rachel, Abraham and Isaac, flood in. We must confront profound questions of faith and belief in the midst of "setbacks, disappointments, even harm" ("Theodicy"). Goostree's poems are a beautiful and deep dive into the nature of agency and powerlessness—the essential question of our epoch and that of every epoch before us.

—Valerie Martínez
author of *Count, Each and Her*, and *Absence, Luminescent*

But There's So Much DIY in IVF That We Can't Be Sure is a lyrical meditation on faith, on how wanting a child is a gesture of hope, and how the inability to conceive a child asks what we do with such powerful love. Toby Goostree's poems are tender and probing investigations into the biblical stories of Leah, Sarah, and Rachel, how children were given to—or withheld from—them as tests, gauges of how much they were loved. "What's the word for intimacy," Goostree writes, "without holding something over you?" Writing as an adoring husband charged with providing fertility shots to his wife, Goostree grapples with this powerlessness, asking, "Will not the judge of earth do right?" This moving collection is both mournful and celebratory, haunting and healing—part love song, part prayer.

—Erin Adair-Hodges
author of *Let's All Die Happy*, and *Every Form of Ruin*

While the nineteenth-century professional schism between art and science persists to this day, Toby Goostree's *But There's So Much DIY in IVF That We Can't Be Sure* reunites the two, not from a practitioner's perspective, à la Williams, but from the patient's. Here Goostree marvels at the language one is forced to learn throughout the IVF process: the hope and longing infused in words like "Novarel" and "antrum," the mysterious-until-too-familiar acronyms, and the distressingly increasing strangeness of "father" and "mother." The speaker occupies a fraught position as both integral to conception and profoundly outside it; unmoored from his religion, his wife, and his community, he turns to poetry to find them all again. This is a book of deep observation and grief, though not without humor and faith.

—Rachel Abramowitz
author of *The Birthday of the Dead*, and *The Puzzle Monster*

for Amy

Contents

"...but Rachel remained childless."
—Genesis 29:31

I.

Impossible

Look up at the sky and count the stars. —Genesis

The first stars were larger
and burned their fuel quickly,

and when they went supernova,
they expelled the elements

they had produced, seeding
the next generation of stars.

Carousel earth, revolving around the sun,
a rolling calendar the years drop off of

—*gone*;

and yet, looking at stars through a telescope,
what you see happened
millions of years ago,

a forthcoming but established fact
and simply empirical,

which Abraham believed.

Anovulation

Six months later, when your period returned
to an empty house, curtains drawn,
I bought an ovulation test;

you were worried you'd see someone we know
and they would know
                    —*what?*

You didn't know.
That first morning the light
under the bathroom door
was like a seam between us, fastening

the news of your test
to what I hoped would follow
—until you opened the door.

This isn't just about sex, you said
days later, turned away

by another empty circle.
But we'd spent the week
we'd been waiting for

in line, waiting. Or that's what it
felt like each morning, our turn
at least another day away,

and with so many others
in front of us, some going through
a second time.

Reticular Activating System

or RAS, is a network of neurons in the brain stem
that modulate behavior, filtering out

unnecessary information while drawing
our attention to what matters,

what we've voluntarily or involuntarily
told our brains to notice.

It's how you have a private conversation
in a loud, crowded restaurant,

or why, when you learn a new word,
you start hearing it everywhere;

it's why a broody couple
notices every baby, both cooing
and crying,

and the parents *at least* as old as they are
with a child that can't be more than—

Moses

When she could no longer hide him or deny
his curiosity, having come to know
him these three months, and fearing Pharaoh's
infanticide, she wrapped him in a papyrus
basket, sealing it, and left him in the Nile
among the reeds, in a place royals would go
to bathe. His sister watched from the bushes, hoping
someone would find him who wanted a child.

I've been waiting in the bushes, too,
watching my wife down by the river.
She's crying. Her shoulders rise as she catches her
breath, carelessly running her hands through
the reeds like a child's hair, a son or daughter,
at her post, an empty basket beside her.

The Kit Arrives

The Styrofoam chest like something
expensive from Legal Sea Foods
—I lift it gingerly,

                 bring it inside. It's light.
Melting of ice will occur during travel.

I remove the top, the Styrofoam creaks,
and a few white flakes fall
to the floor.

              Two bags of syringes, needles,
and alcohol swabs line the surface.
Then something called Follistim Pen,

microfine needles and Q-Caps, boxes of Ganirelex,
a vial of Novarel, boxes of Follistim
and Menopur stacked at the bottom.

I call to tell her the package arrived,
everything is taken care of,
the right items

             refrigerated, and I hear
her body relax like we're here together,

but she can't see it yet, how much of it there is,
so I say I'm working late so that she will.

Follistim Pen

I unscrew the cartridge holder
from the body of the pen
in order to load it.

I set the body aside;
—detached, it looks like
a mascara wand. You

-Tube cleans the rubber stopper
on the Follistim cartridge
with an alcohol swab

and then inserts it,
getting ahead with every step,
my mind buffering

always. More steps
until the pen is loaded.

—I tap the cartridge and a tear swells
at the tip of the needle, ready to burst.

This releases air, ensuring
the right amount of dosage,

though there's so much DIY in IVF
that we can't be sure.

Beside herself, Amy watches.

The Blessing

*... and there wrestled a man with him until
the breaking of the day.* —Genesis

A man came upon Jacob in prayer and put
him in a headlock, and when he wrestled free,
the man tried to use a single leg takedown, but
Jacob was too quick.

                —Oh, choreography
of prayer, the surprise half-nelson of it
as we're dragged from ourselves. Or pinned, like Jacob.
Why did we kneel? Why did we close our eyes if
not to be vulnerable?

Father

His posture leaning against a rail,
right ankle crossed
over my left

like a shoe being tied,
an unconscious half-curtsy.

Or, interrupted,
taking my glasses off
to talk, then putting them

back on to read, reading
and talking it out

like I'm disclaiming
the information.

Climbing a flight of stairs,
I can hear
our steps together,

his creak and click
in mine;

coming across a chair left
out for someone
in the kitchen or study,

a chair that someone
forgot to tuck back in,
I tip it forward—

supplicant against the table,
reserved, not for my father

to rejoin me
or a son to replace me

but for every other seat
between us.

if

the dopamine-related
areas of the brain

active in the newly smitten
are also active

well into marriage
if it's good

as recent research holds
what a windfall

for both body and spirit
for happy couples

what a rebuttal

to the fear of rushing in
or exhausting dopamine

to get to love

Femara

essentially inhibits the enzyme
aromatase, which suppresses estrogen,
prompting the brain and pituitary gland
to increase the output of FSH,

follicle stimulating hormone. This
can result in the development of
a mature follicle in the ovary
and ovulation of an egg,

whereas prayer

Sin

If you satisfy, *why?*
               Maybe you don't
or, by the time you do, we've given up?
Like a view that takes too long to develop
or the right words afterward. Shouldn't. *Won't*—
until I do again. Then back to the station
for processing and the one-man lineup.
Back for good? I can only laugh, chin up
like I could make bail with pocket change.

Before I know it's Tuesday, I know it's you.
And while I'm thankful for the chance to talk
face-to-face in a prison cubicle
with glass between us—*forgive my tone.*
This glass that lets me see what Moses couldn't
—*panim*, your face—still catches light, reflection.

Uniform

A nurse slips out through the corner curtain vent,
and Amy undresses, stepping into
a powder-blue gown
                              that I tie in back.

Out of context,
out of form-fitting clothes,
her body is just a body, off the rack, anyone's,
which makes this more intimate.

Outside, indoor voices; the intermittent breeze
of bodies headed elsewhere, triaged,
brushing us off in their wake

—until a nurse enters, introduces herself
as Eve.
            After a list of questions
and another explanation of egg retrieval,

she tries to administer an IV
in the most conspicuous vein
at the joint of Amy's right arm.

Mild track marks line it already:
several weeks' worth of daily blood.
Catnip, Amy says,
                              and Eve laughs

but then fails with the best choice
in both arms and says she'll bring in Lauren
because *she's really good at this.*

But Lauren isn't better,
                              or the result is the same
as they pivot back and
forth, on both sides of Amy's body,

trying again in the arm, then at each wrist,
before settling on the top
of her left hand, which works.

You aren't fluffy like some of them
Eve says, *fluffy* her word for weight;

and I see it, the charm on her name badge,
a single sperm, probably a joke at first
now part of her uniform,
                              a tadpole so *amphibious*

—able to walk away.

Faith

Your map app drains my battery
through a suburb of small corrections,

stop signs and speedbumps,
like I'm set to avoid
                    highways and tolls;

you send me down a road
without service
or with only two bars,

preferring the long conversation
of road when I only want to arrive;

and your way supplies any
backseat driver
                    with another way

of second-guessing me,
and I'm giving them more.

The Rest of the Time

At our church, on weeks where
someone in the congregation
has had a baby, a rose sits in a vase
on top of the piano. Pastor Glenn
will mention the family, introducing
the baby by name, and people usually
clap, sometimes at length, depending
on who the new parents are. It's nice;
—*it's still nice*, though now I see it missing
on Sundays where there is no rose.

II.

Flood

... their days will be a hundred and twenty years. —Genesis

Unburdened, one hundred twenty years
to recant; but when the ground burst—there

is only afterward and ever since.
Riddance of the great abyss, catharsis

in a swirl of cries and kicking; and rain,
weeks of it, anger finding bottom in

heaps of bones wedged into coral. The ark
a dinghy drifting without hope of port.

The destruction was just, when I
bother to think of it, more interested by

what you kept—two of every kind. Given
food, water. A place to wait out water. As if

you weren't yet ready to start over,
preferring the way things are.

The End of the Day

Things begin and end apart from each other.
I think we can agree on that.
From the dead-lift grunt of the garage door
we know not to account for the day's invisible clutter.

And I think we can agree that,
once you've asked the question, it's already over—
no one can account for the day's invisible clutter,
the squeaks across the hardwood floor.

Because once you've asked the question, it's already over—
the day was fine; I hope the night will be better.
I need a minute to negotiate the shifting floor
which isn't the same as wanting the night to be over.

The day was fine, I know the night will be better.
We'll keep busy by coming up with things to do
so that we'll both be sorry when the night is over
in a mutual way we can't admit to.

We'll keep busy by coming up with things to do
because we're so afraid that we don't fulfill the other
in a mutual way we can't admit to.
We are distracted during our time together.

We're both so afraid that we don't fulfill the other
that, like a hidden end nail scratching a pocket door,
distraction catches us brushing against each other.
Things begin and end apart from each other.

Ultrasound

Cycle Day 3

As they mature, the follicles gain
a fluid-filled cavity

known as the antrum;
antral follicles

are large enough to count
via a transvaginal ultrasound.

Between eight and fiften follicles
is considered acceptable,

and a cycle may be canceled
if the count is too low,

but when Amy returns,
it's like they spread the gel
across her mind

to show what she's thinking:
not just a follicle of hope but a hive.

Sperm Sample

The light impression of the last person
left in the BarcaLounger

like that of a head you'd wipe off a pillow

                             —nurse!

A fresh key before the room was ready,
I go through everything:

the cup, plastic-wrapped,
plucked from a bin in the supply room

like a fortune cookie,
whichever is on top;

the paperwork, a no-nonsense cop of
license and registration and when did you last ejaculate?

Pornography,

centerfolds where a selfie would do
more, or imagination.

                         Facing me, a DVD player
and—*in my hand, already?*—a remote.
Low-tech appendage.

I hear a voice outside the room
or in my head. Exchanging the remote
for my phone,
                  I take a seat.

Motility.

Concentration.

Two of the few medical words I know.

I know;

as if my only thought of climate change
is the sight of myself in sunglasses.

A friend says
the problem with *his* shame
is that it's all about him,

more screen time for having done wrong.

—*My phone agrees,*

inured to adult sites for the length of
the next few minutes,
or the built-in one-year warranty.

Longer!

NSFW? But it *is* work.
Just ask the actors,

endlessly grooming their pubic hair
to the razor's edge of a keyword search

—*the maintenance*—
and mine a dust bowl picking up gray.

Hands

at ten and two, 1996;

soon overconfident,
down to one at noon,
sometimes six,

neck reining across the left lane
through traffic,

my gearshift's knob a saddle's horn.
I loped for miles, *years*

according to an
unbroken Mustang's odometer.

on Turning Forty

Back is Best

or has been
since the American Academy of Pediatrics
put your babies down for a nap

more than a decade ago,
reducing the risk of SIDS;

but some wake with flat spots
on the back of their heads,

plagiocephaly,
soft skull flattened like resting dough.

So our friends do tummy time
with their babies
to promote rolling over,

~~before drop-off~~, after pickup,
on weekends whenever they can

—*whenever they can*
rolling over us.

Rachels

When the Lord saw that Leah was not loved,
he enabled her to conceive. —Genesis

In lieu of a flu shot, *antivenom?*
Because I need a reason less generous
than *that—*
                when the Lord saw that Leah
was not loved. What would be one?
                                                    If she was

loved, not just provided for. *Even if*
she wasn't loved, provided *as its own*
reward. On purpose. *For—*
                                        no what-ifs,
buts, or ors. If sex wasn't her only

power, or if it was stronger: no doctors.
—Doctors! If Clomid, Femara, Follistim,
Menopur. If mourning-noon-and-night.

                                        —Longer!

If *in*efficient, slow; involved, firsthand

—proof! insofar as beauty can be, of what
happens where love *is,*
                                without instruction.

After the Surgery to Remove My Diseased Left Eye

The light from my father's laptop
was like a light inside a window
he was looking in—

compelling, one-sided,
its glow fading across his face like breath.
And he must have been behind at work

because he typed so fast, without
any pause for spaces,

as if a single, unpronounceable word
had been building up for weeks,
and he was going to get it out.

When he finally did, and the typing stopped,
I was ready for him to leave my room.
But even after the screen went dark,

he couldn't look away from it,
his damp fingers slipping toward
the keyboard's ledge

as the laptop balanced on his knees.
And the longer he looked, the more
I wanted to see what he did,

his blank screen a dark window now,
his glassy eyes dilated shut.

*

I've been blind in my left eye since birth,
so with my second prosthetic, like the one before,
it's not about what I see but how I look.

This left eye looks better than the last one did,
but it's awkward when people point that out
like I've had something caught in my teeth
for almost a decade.

*

A bottle of Visine—*artificial tears*.
There wasn't a dry eye in that house

except mine,

lubricated, self-medicated,
half-empties everywhere.

What did I expect? A pair of eyes,
looking in the same direction?
Impossible,

unless I'm looking straight ahead
like a set of headlights.

*

Instead of a phantom limb,
I imagine a scab,

blocking germs, giving my skin
underneath a chance to heal;

—brown like dormant grass,
I forget the skin is coming back,

but after a few weeks of care,
of water, of washing,

the skin is green across my body
of land, so lush, so deep,

I can't tell what's been mowed
from what hasn't.

The Second Sunday

the Lord God banished him from the Garden of Eden —Genesis

After the seventh day caesura rest,
when your tracks were fresh and easy to follow,
your intention firmly rooted
                              —what else?
The sun stood by its initial glow,

burning like its own idea. In eagles and plankton,
predator and prey, you soared and drifted,
gaining nourishment and being eaten.
Life itself, a part of you, insisted

on by *life itself*. Like a word repeated
in its definition. Everywhere your
best ideas. Everything already,
including death: *animal skins*. Cover for

corrupted bodies, disabused of sin
too late:
            insight, outside the garden.

Night Feeding

for mothers

Sleep, *sleep*, colostrum of new mothers,
latched to the white noise of a baby monitor.

Tower of Babel

Emboldened, round-the-clock they work together,
coy as a weathervane's point-of-view
—until *you*, the general contractor, return
to check their work. Coup d'état meet coup

de grâce. *Ahh*—subs. Willful to the studs.
REPLENISH THE EARTH. You think *suburbs*, right?
BE FRUITFUL AND MULTIPLY. You think kids.
Kids. You can't stop them, but you can make it

harder; and if you could speak to each one
differently, apart from the others—word
gets around. Comparing bids, talk of a union;
never without suspicion or their brothers

around, as different loopholes in the same
tower impart distinct views, but affiliate.

Dr. Marsh Says

we can freeze any extra embryos
until we're ready again, if ever

if, any; extra

uneven shoulder yoke
of hopelessness and hope,

one bucket empty, the other full
between us.

Twenty eggs were fertilized.
Twenty! I can remember thinking

leaving the rest behind,
will I be like the novelist

who identifies with his characters,
even stifling them, especially in drafts?

I can remember thinking
we can't give them away,

inviting plagiarism,
when our house is full of books.

Only two survived
to move forward with genetic testing.

III.

at abels grave

my eye is drawn to him
or the back of him
standing before the rest
like an example
fathers who lost their sons
after he did
is there a word for them
its worse than widower
i could read it on their lips
but they won't turn around

Faith

The Lord did for Sarah what he had promised. —*Genesis*

Once, Sarah liked having friends
who knew and friends who didn't,
outlets and dams

to direct a steady flow of hope.
When she would feel a letdown
coming, she'd pull her shawl across

her chest without thinking.
But her breasts were empty,
and she felt envy

at new mothers' milk stains,
disabused of shame,
unaware of their good luck.

Who would have believed what they see now?
New wine in old wineskins, ready to burst.

Running Over

Wobbling down our street on my first bike,
a red Schwinn, my first religion,

encouraged to go faster but afraid
of falling, chasing balance,

wanting both to impress my dad
and to run him over,

as he backed away as I rode toward him

not in retreat but to pull the finish line
farther away. *The problem with a father dying*

is that there's no one left in front of you.

But if that front row to dread
would make room for another

so that my dad is actually blocking progress
just by living,
killing my chance of a son,

then I worry that he'll live forever,
even as I can't let on

—or else he'd hold his ground,
no longer backing away from me

or safe
when I come.

Even CCs

Of the embryos that have formed,
typically one third will survive five to seven days
to become blastocysts.
                              Survivors
are graded based on quality.
Their scores determine

if they should be implanted
as well as the order of implantation

if more than one qualifies. AAs are
the highest quality,
                              though doctors
will still implant ABs, BBs, BCs, and
even CCs—
                  the leftover blastocysts.

His Body of Laundry

Reaching in through Isaac's toddler sleeve,
inside out, damp still, mostly cuff at this age,

Sarah redirects it like she's dressing him,
gently restoring the arm down his side

indefinitely, as long as he lets her.

Theodicy

I'm not asking for proof or an alibi,
but when your name comes up at accidents
it would help to know what we're dealing with—
wind that got away? The fact of ice,

black ice even, as risks crystallize?
Or is it *us*? As if the precipice
isn't there until we look down; as if
—*what*? Doubt could add risk. So could denial:

*Wild*fires? Natural disasters? Or the avalanche
of setbacks, disappointments, even harm.
Acquit yourself! Dismiss the charges!
Or, when you judge, call me to the bench.

Put your hand over the mic so the others
won't hear, and you won't have to whisper.

for Mark Walters

Only Child

after Isaac

Unless the neighbor siblings are stuck at
a game of three-square, someone short

of an even number no matter how odd;
on standby,

and the waiting list of a school
where tuition limits parents

to a single child, a small class size
at home.

                    Can you imagine?

No bunk beds, no middle seat;
space, but no room for error.
No brothers or sisters,
                              shadow's foil;

a person described in third person
who sets an example
                    without needing to.

Trigger Shot

At 11:45 p.m.,
I insert the syringe into the Novarel,
flip the vial upside down, and pull

the plunger back like the string of a bow,

handing it to Amy
to shoot an arrow into night.

The Scratch

At the *fin de siècle* of a long IVF cycle
la fin du monde for us,
in a foreign language,

                    for me vicarious,
though I try to understand because of Amy.

She has the scratch to prove it
didn't work,

              a provocation

across the lining of her womb
to get a reaction, chemicals and hormones

racing to her defense so that
this injury might make her endometrium

more receptive to an embryo.

I love her endometrium;
—I love her body,

not as a source of information
or as a tool

              but as a lover,

and as a husband given to action,
triage, putting her first.

Which is why I can't see past her,
leaving the future out of focus,

smudged like day-old henna

—I can't see a baby
for her, for us.

Oh, foolish plans!
Oh, smug house in a good school district!

You premature tattoos.

I regret, but I don't regret you
across my chest, down my back
and even up my neck,

so I have to explain you to others.

Those Sunday Nights

Street light, falling without accumulating
though it was winter;

and herringbone across the airport parking lot,
half-empty, familiar,
faint through salt and weather.

A few dark cars exhaled smoke
between drags of cold, November air;
I held my breath as long as you did.

With only so many left,
with just a few minutes
—but we didn't think like that in college,

our noses turned up to time,
our next rendezvous two weeks away.

When a plane's nose points slightly upward,
aerodynamics begin to change.

At high altitudes, where the atmosphere is thin,
further ascent can disrupt
the smooth flow of air over a plane's wings.

The plane's lift, the force of physics
that pulls it into the sky

because there's less pressure above the wings
than below them, can deteriorate

and, in extreme conditions,
cause an aerodynamic stall,

a situation in which a plane starts falling,
even as its engines strain with thrust
and its nose points skyward,

thousands more feet to fall
fourteen years into marriage.

Deus Ex Machina

Take your son, your only son, whom you love ...
Sacrifice him as a burnt offering. —Genesis

Giving the instruction felt like doubling
back in front of you,
                              freely caught

walking back my word. Doubling back,
overlap—what's the word for intimacy
without holding something over you?

What's the word if I do?

You didn't understand. How could you?
And Sarah had so many questions

that she didn't know to ask. How could you
leave without telling her?
                              In good faith,
without encouragement, you left her
room for faith with an early start.

*

Mount Moriah.

Leaving hope at basecamp with the servants
and the donkeys
                    who watched them walk away,

Isaac looks defeated; *I should have told him.*
But it's just until they see the ram.

When Abraham comes to the place
he'll raise his hand
                    —if it comes to that—

but surely his faith will be depleted, flaccid, even,
short of a miracle—

Is worship persuasive?
                    Is it meant to be?
Wearing a hair shirt of skin with empty pockets?
But I am a God of grace.

He's laid Isaac on the altar.
                    The boy looks

pathetic, no tribute, and yet
he isn't fighting like the ram will;

he's accepted it, how it's the same
in the long run.
                    And yet, men don't really *have*

wasted years; some even prefer it
—getting established—

though their wives may
suffer, waiting for children. Sarah did,
which means Abraham did,
                              even if he didn't.

But he *did. Ishmael.* So insecure,
so unsure of his place in the family.

Impossible to please.

Abraham would have him over
but, after an hour,
                            he'd ask to leave.

Defensive of him with Sarah, critical
of him with Hagar,
                            Abraham made it worse.

—*Oh Abraham.* I'm hungry.

What's taking so long?
The ram is ready. Why isn't Isaac bound?

But I shouldn't rush them; they think
they're saying goodbye.
                            I want to ask

Will not the judge of earth do right?

Like when I agreed *not* to destroy
the wicked city for 50 righteous men

—or 45, or 40, or 30, or 20, or 10—
when Abraham interceded.

But how much more for 9-8-7-6-5-4-3-2 or 1?
I asked him. He replied,

What about the unborn? Oh, Abraham!

By the time Isaac understands *that,*
we'll be long gone,

but at this higher altitude,
equally close to death

                in my imagination,

we're intragenerational, like-minded,
looking in the same direction

—except that Isaac is bound,

                   and I will never die.

But *you're* holding the knife.

                 You're stretching out your hand—

Abraham! Abraham!

But as he raises his eyes to see the ram,
I can see myself

           as I watch him

drive the blade like a fist into Isaac,
an offering for sin

              to bring us back together

even as I pull away from him, *horrified*,
but also needing to *look* horrified

as if this isn't what I wanted.
It's not. We'll never speak again.

I'll abandon what I can,

                letting nature run its course,

without Isaac, or Jacob, or Judah or
—he isn't listening.

He's kneeling over Isaac.
His lips are moving,
                    belying prayer,

but the ram is restless, and all
I hear is bleating, *bleating*

for dried blades or just an ear of grain
or pasture.

IV.

January

For months you circled
days on a calendar
as we tried to direct desire
like a balloon in flight,

rising, retreating
until we could no longer see it
looking up.

When Noah cracked the hatch
in the ark's roof,
he released a dove,

but she returned because
water still covered the earth.
He tried again

a week later, and she came back
with an olive branch
in her mouth.

What if desire returns
just to be released again
as the dove was

or, ultimately,
like a group of balloons
may have to be—

in unison, in memory
of a missing child
after the search is called off?

Acknowledgments

Many thanks to the following journals in which these poems appeared, sometimes in different form:

The Cincinnati Review: The Blessing

The Midwest Quarterly: The Scratch

Christianity and Literature: Theodicy

Santa Clara Review: Moses

Harbor Review: Rachels

Tar River Review: Faith

Kansas City Voices: The End of the Day

The Windhover: Impossible, Sin

I-70 Review: After the Surgery to Review My Diseased Left
   Eye, Uniform

Tomorrow and Tomorrow: Dr. Marsh Says, Only Child

Anglican Theological Review: Flood

Maryland Literary Review: Anovulation, Follistim Pen

Pittsburgh Poetry Review: The Kit, Trigger Shot, January

By and By Poetry: Those Sunday Nights

Jewish Literary Review: Father, The Second Sunday

I'd like to thank Eric Muhr and the staff at Fernwood Press for bringing my book into the world.

I'd like to thank the poets who workshopped the manuscript at the Taos Writer's Conference and a Tupelo Manuscript Conference.

I'm grateful to Valerie Martinez, David Rigsbee, Jennifer Michael Hecht, Rachel Abramowitz, Boyer Rickel, Erin Adair-Hodges, Devon Ewing, and Jeffrey Levine for their close readings of the manuscript.

Thanks to my friends who believed without proof: Thomas McGannon, Tim Cooper, Paul Raccuglia, Ryan Bisel, Jake Hendershot, Adam Benton, Matt and Libby Gertken.

I'd like to thank Grant Cansler for taking the manuscript seriously, often bringing it up, even in public. I'd like to thank Gabe Egli for his thinking around Deus Ex Machina, bringing his ideas to bear on mine, much to my benefit.

I'd like to thank Berit Lindboe for her impact on my life. You've never stopped teaching because you've never stopped learning.

I'd like to thank my mom and dad for a house full of ideas and support.

I'm indebted to Mark Walters for his tireless devotion to the manuscript, rereading so many drafts, and for his example, itself a draft of the writer's life, one I read and reread for insight and direction.

Amy, I was spoken for the moment you said my name. We gave everything we had and got more in return: Jack. *Jack.*

Notes

In "Running Over," the line *the problem with a father dying is that there's no one left in front of you* is lifted from Martin Amis' 2000 interview with Charlie Rose focused on his memoir, *Experience*, and his relationship with his father, Kingsley.

In "Those Sunday Nights," the description of aerodynamics comes from Chapter 3 of Charles Duhigg's *Smarter Better Faster: The Transformative Power of Real Productivity*.

www.ingramcontent.com/pod-product-compliance
Lightning Source LLC
Chambersburg PA
CBHW010858090426
42737CB00020B/3413